It's fun to draw Monsters

Mark Bergin

Author:
Mark Bergin was born in Hastings, England. He has illustrated an award winning series and written over twenty books. He has done many book designs, layouts and storyboards in many styles including cartoon for numerous books, posters and adverts. He lives in Bexhill-on-sea with his wife and three children.

Editorial Assistant:
Rob Walker

HOW TO USE THIS BOOK:
Start by following the numbered splats on the left hand page. These steps will ask you to add some lines to your drawing. The new lines are always drawn in red so you can see how the drawing builds from step to step. Read the 'You can do it!' splats to learn about drawing and colouring techniques you can use.

Published in Great Britain in MMXII by Scribblers, a division of Book House
25 Marlborough Place, Brighton BN1 1UB
www.salariya.com
www.book-house.co.uk

ISBN-13: 978-1-908177-60-5

1 3 5 7 9 8 6 4 2

A CIP catalogue record for this book is available from the British Library.

Printed and bound in China.

PAPER FROM
SUSTAINABLE
FORESTS

Visit our website at **www.book-house.co.uk** or go to **www.salariya.com** for **free** electronic versions of:
You Wouldn't Want to be an Egyptian Mummy!
You Wouldn't Want to be a Roman Gladiator!
You Wouldn't Want to be a Polar Explorer!
You Wouldn't Want to Sail on a 19th-Century Whaling Ship!

Visit our Bookhouse 100 channel to see Mark Bergin doing step by step illustrations:

www.youtube.com/user/BookHouse100

Contents

Klawz

1 Start with the head shape. Add a mouth and teeth.

2 Draw in two eyes on each side of the head and add hair.

Splat-a-fact
Monsters have very sharp teeth and claws.

You can do it!
Use wax crayons to create texture and paint over it with watercolour paint. Use felt-tip for the lines.

3 Draw a triangle for the body and add an oval shape. Draw in the legs.

4

4 Draw in four more legs with feet and claws.

Fangor

1 Start by cutting the body shape out of orange card. Stick down.

2 Cut out the head and the teeth and stick down. Draw in the eye and mouth.

MAKE SURE YOU GET AN ADULT TO HELP YOU WHEN USING SCISSORS!

you can do it!

Cut out the shapes from coloured paper. Stick these on to a sheet of blue paper. Use felt-tip for the lines.

Splat-a-fact

This monster is very good at juggling.

3 Cut out shapes for the horns and feet and stick down.

4 Cut out the arms and spots for the body. Stick down.

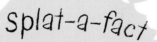
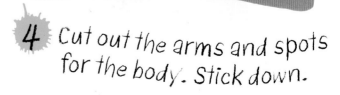

6

Fuzzbit

1 Start with this jagged shape for the head. Add one large eye.

2 Draw in the mouth then add a jagged line for the body.

Splat-a-fact
Monsters are as strong as nine men.

You can do it!
Use a felt-tip for the lines. Add colour with a variety of coloured pencils.

3 Draw in two large feet with claws.

4 Add the arms and hands.

spindle

1 Start with a circle and add a mouth.

2 Draw in four eyeballs on stalks.

3 Draw in the nostrils and teeth and add a dot to each eyeball.

you can do it!
Use a blue felt-tip for the lines and colour in with different coloured felt-tips.

Splat-a-fact
Some monsters are very funny and like to tell jokes.

4 Add the arms.

5 Draw in three legs.

10

Grunty

1 Draw in the main body. Add a big eye and a small eye.

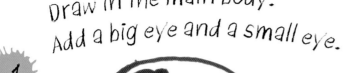

2 Draw circles for spots and add dots to the eyes. Add a mouth.

you can do it!

Use a felt-tip for the lines. Add colour with wax crayons.

3 Add the legs, feet and middle antenna.

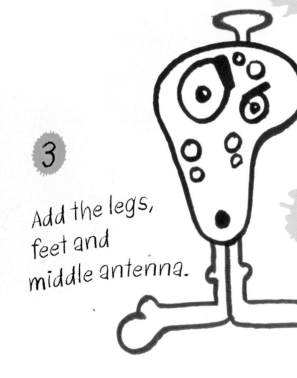

Splat-a-fact

Monsters can hear very well with their antennae.

4 Draw in another two antennae. Add two arms.

12

Rangledorf

1 Draw in the spiky body.

2 Add the eyes, mouth and teeth.

you can do it!
Use a felt-tip for the lines. For extra effect, paint in ink washes, adding a touch of coloured ink to areas that are still wet.

Splat-a-fact
Some monsters make loud, scary, roaring sounds.

3 Draw four legs.

4 Add the horns, two arms and claws.

14

Oculus

1 Start with an oval shape. Add a large mouth with three big teeth.

2 Add three claws.

splat-a-fact
This monster lives underground.

3 Add lots of eyes.

you can do it!
Use a felt-tip for the lines and then add colour with watercolour paints. Use a sponge to dab on more colour to create texture.

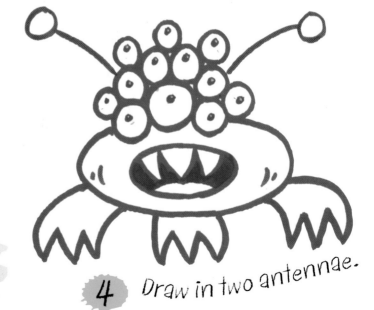

4 Draw in two antennae.

16

Blarp

1 Start by drawing this shape. Add a mouth.

2 Draw in one large eye and a row of teeth.

you can do it!

Use wax crayons for texture and paint over it with watercolour paint. Use a felt-tip for the lines.

3 Add little hands and feet.

Splat- a fact

This monster can hover in the air.

4 Draw in the horns and antennae.

Gizzard

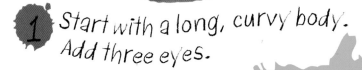

1 Start with a long, curvy body. Add three eyes.

2 Add the mouth, teeth, ears and hair.

you can do it!
Use coloured pencils. Try putting textured surfaces under your paper to create interesting effects.

Splat-a-fact
This monster has seven legs and three eyes!

3 Draw in seven legs with circles for feet.

4 Add stripes and draw in spikes and a heart-shaped tail.

Oddlin

1 Cut out this shape from coloured tissue paper and stick down.

you can do it!
Cut the shapes from coloured tissue paper and glue in place. Use a felt-tip for the lines.

MAKE SURE YOU GET AN ADULT TO HELP YOU WHEN USING SCISSORS!

2 Draw in one eye, a mouth and teeth.

3 Cut out the shapes for two large feet and stick down.

4 Draw in two arms. Tear out pieces of tissue paper to decorate the body. Stick down.

Fijjit

1 Start with this shape and add two eyes.

2 Add details to the eyes and a line of sharp teeth.

3 Draw in the horns and finish off the mouth.

Splat-a-fact
Monsters can run super-fast.

4 Add the arms and claws.

You can do it!
Use wax crayons for texture and paint over it with watercolour paint. Use a felt-tip for the lines.

5 Draw the legs and feet.

25

Krungo

1 Start with a spiky body.

2 Add two dots for nostrils, a mouth and teeth.

you can do it!
Use a felt-tip for the lines. Add colour with chalky pastels. and blend the colours with your fingers.

Splat-a-fact
This monster is great at climbing trees.

3 Add a striped horn, two eyes and feet.

4 Add the arms and claws.

27

splazz

1 Start with this shape. Add a mouth.

2 Add three eyes.

you can do it!
Use a graphite pencil for the lines and add colour using watercolour paints.

Splat-a-fact
Some monsters live underwater.

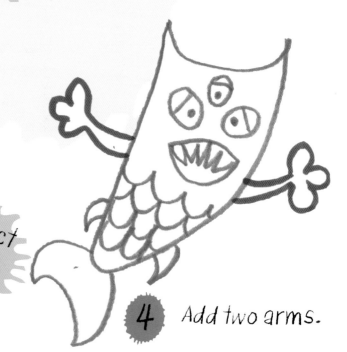

4 Add two arms.

3 Add jagged teeth, scales, a tail and fins.

Prootle

1 Start with the head shape. Add a mouth and teeth.

2 Draw in three eyes, horns and ears.

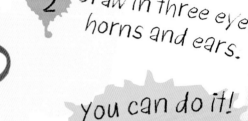

Splat-a-fact
Monsters can sleep with their eyes open.

you can do it!
Use a felt-tip for the lines, then use soft pastels for the colours and blend with your finger.

3 Draw in the body and add lots of spots.

4 Draw in the arms and legs.

Index

FREE APP!

Download our free iPhone and iPad catalogue app. Search for Salariya or Book House

Available on the App Store

Children's non-fiction and graphic novels

www.salariya.com
where books come to life!

The Salariya Book Company is a UK-based independent publisher of books for children which sells both domestically and internationally. Through our imprints Book House, Scribblers and Scribo we are dedicated to publishing books with real child appeal, using innovative concepts, high-quality illustrations, informative writing and, above all, humour to captivate the minds of young people. With a mind for the environment, all of our books are printed on paper from sustainable forests. Click the links below to visit our imprints' websites, read our Book House Blog or dive into a world of free interactive web books from the best-selling 'You Wouldn't Want To Be...' series.

The Salariya Book Company,
25, Marlborough Place,
Brighton,
East Sussex
BN1 1UB
England
United Kingdom

Tel: 01273 603306
Fax: 01273 621619

rights - www.murray@salariya.com
press - jamie.pitman@salariya.com
editorial - stephen.haynes@salariya.com
managing director - david@salariya.com

Scribblers
Bright Start

FREE WEB BOOK!

Scribo fiction

Fiction for children and teenagers

Free activities, puzzles and web books, with information about our books for babies, toddlers and pre-school

Follow us on Facebook and Twitter

www.youtube.com/user/BookHouse100

THE BOOK HOUSE BLOG

The Book House blog - competitions, giveaways and current news

Four free web books

FREE WEB BOOKS!